All New Cookie Dough Fun

Publications International, Ltd.

Recipe Development on pages 18, 20, 22, 24, 26, 29, 32, 34, 40, 42, 44, 49, 52, 56 and 58 by Dari Carré and Betsy Oppenneer, CCP.

Front cover photography and photography on pages 19, 21, 23, 25, 27, 31, 33, 35, 41, 43, 45, 51, 53, 57 and 59 by Sanders Studios, Inc.

Photographer: Kathy Sanders
Photographer's Assistants: Cristin Nestor and Kathy Ores
Prop Stylist: Patty Higgins
Food Stylists: Carol Parik, Teri Rys-Maki, Mary-Helen Steindler
Assistant Food Stylist: Julie Morris

Pictured on front and back cover: *(clockwise from top):* Choo-choo Train *(page 29),* Lady Bugs *(page 44),* Crayon Cookies *(page 42),* Butterfly Cookies *(page 52),* Dude Ranch *(page 26),* Under the Sea *(page 24),* Baseball Caps *(page 56)* and Cookie Tools *(page 34).*

ISBN: 0-7853-3552-8

Manufactured in U.S.A.

8 7 6 5 4 3 2 1

Microwave Cooking: Microwave ovens vary in wattage. Use the cooking times as guidelines and check for doneness before adding more time.

All New Cookie Dough Fun

COOKIE DOUGH MANIA

Capture the moment with cookies. Travel through the pages of this whimsical magazine and discover dozens of magical ways to use cookie dough to make all of your child's cookie fantasies come true. Dazzle your favorite cookie monster with creative cookie treats or keep their minds and little hands busy for hours exploring their own imagination with every cookie decoration. It has never been easier to add some fun to brown-bag lunches, after-school snacks and all your children's parties.

- All cookie dough should be well chilled before using. Unless the recipe states otherwise, work with the recommended portion of dough called for and refrigerate the remaining dough until needed.

- Follow recipe directions and baking times. Check for doneness using the test given in the recipe.

- Most refrigerated cookie dough expands considerably when baked. Always leave two inches between cookies when placing them on cookie sheets.

General Guidelines

- Measure all the ingredients and assemble them in the order called for in the recipe.

Supplies:

Some of the recipes in *All New Cookie Dough Fun* call for special equipment or nonfood items; these are always listed in the recipe under the heading

"Supplies." Most of the supplies listed are available in stores carrying cake decorating equipment and in supermarkets. Additional equipment you may need includes a pastry brush, lollipop sticks, cardboard and pastry bags and decorating tips.

Kitchen Equipment:

Equipment not listed under "Supplies" are items typically found in a well-equipped kitchen: mixing bowls, cookie and baking sheets, rolling pins, saucepans, aluminum foil, waxed paper and cookie cutters.

Special Techniques

Making Patterns:

When a pattern is to be used only once, as for the Choo-choo Train (page 29), make the pattern out of waxed paper. Using the diagram(s) and photo as guides, draw the pattern pieces on waxed paper. Cut the pieces out and place them on the cookie. Cut around the pattern pieces with a sharp knife. Remove the pattern pieces and discard. Continue as directed in the recipe.

For patterns that are used more than once, make the pattern more durable by using clean, lightweight cardboard or poster board. Using the diagram(s) and photo as guides, draw the pattern pieces on the cardboard. Cut the pieces out and lightly spray one side with nonstick cooking spray. Place pattern pieces, sprayed side down, on the rolled-out dough and cut around them with a sharp knife. Reuse the pattern pieces to make as many cutouts as needed.

Tinting Coconut:

Dilute a few drops of food coloring with ½ teaspoon water in a large plastic food storage bag. Add 1 to 1⅓ cups flaked coconut. Close the bag and shake well until the coconut is evenly coated. If a deeper color is desired, add more diluted food coloring and shake again.

Be Creative

Let your imagination go wild— decorate your way! Use the decorations, suggestions and photos as a starting point to set you on your way. Let your creative flair show. Feel free to change colors or shapes to suit your family or party. The White Decorator Frosting on page 22 can always be used instead of purchased frosting; simply tint it to create all the shades you desire. Most importantly—have fun!

CHILD'S PLAY

Cheery Chocolate Animal Cookies

What you need:

1 (10-ounce) package REESE'S® Peanut Butter Chips
1 cup HERSHEY'S Semi-Sweet Chocolate Chips
2 tablespoons shortening *(do not use butter, margarine or oil)*
1 package (20 ounces) chocolate sandwich cookies
1 package (10 ounces) animal crackers

1   Line trays or cookie sheets with waxed paper.

2   In 2-quart glass measuring cup with handle, combine chips and shortening. Microwave on HIGH (100% power) 1½ to 2 minutes or until chips are melted and mixture is smooth when stirred.

3   With fork, dip each cookie into melted chip mixture; gently tap fork on side of cup to remove excess chocolate. Place chocolate-coated cookies on prepared trays; top each cookie with an animal cracker. Chill until chocolate is set, about 30 minutes. Store in airtight container in a cool, dry place.
Makes about 4 dozen cookies

Cheery Chocolate Animal Cookies

Brownie Turtle Cookies

What you need:

2 squares (1 ounce each) unsweetened baking chocolate
⅓ cup solid vegetable shortening
1 cup granulated sugar
½ teaspoon vanilla extract
2 large eggs
1¼ cups all-purpose flour
½ teaspoon baking powder
½ teaspoon salt
1 cup "M&M's"® Milk Chocolate Mini Baking Bits, divided
1 cup pecan halves
⅓ cup caramel ice cream topping
⅓ cup shredded coconut
⅓ cup finely chopped pecans

1 Preheat oven to 350°F. Lightly grease cookie sheets; set aside.

2 Heat chocolate and shortening in 2-quart saucepan over low heat, stirring constantly until melted; remove from heat. Mix in sugar, vanilla and eggs. Blend in flour, baking powder and salt. Stir in ⅔ cup "M&M's"® Milk Chocolate Mini Baking Bits.

3 For each cookie, arrange 3 pecan halves, with ends almost touching at center, on prepared cookie sheets. Drop dough by rounded teaspoonfuls onto center of each group of pecans; mound the dough slightly.

4 Bake 8 to 10 minutes just until set. Do not overbake. Cool completely on wire racks.

5 In small bowl combine ice cream topping, coconut and nuts; top each cookie with about 1½ teaspoons mixture. Press remaining ⅓ cup "M&M's"® Milk Chocolate Mini Baking Bits into topping.

Makes about 2½ dozen cookies

Kids' Favorite Jumbo Chippers

What you need:

1 cup (2 sticks) butter, softened
¾ cup granulated sugar
¾ cup packed brown sugar
2 eggs
1 teaspoon vanilla
2¼ cups all-purpose flour
1 teaspoon baking soda
¾ teaspoon salt
1 package (9 ounces) candy-coated chocolate pieces
1 cup peanut butter flavored chips

1 Preheat oven to 375°F.

2 Beat butter, granulated sugar and brown sugar in large bowl until light and fluffy. Beat in eggs and vanilla. Add flour, baking soda and salt. Beat until well blended. Stir in chocolate pieces and peanut butter chips. Drop by rounded tablespoonfuls 3 inches apart onto ungreased cookie sheets.

3 Bake 10 to 12 minutes or until edges are golden brown. Let cookies stand on cookie sheets 2 minutes. Remove cookies to wire racks; cool completely.

Makes 3 dozen cookies

Tip: *For a change of pace, substitute white chocolate chips, chocolate chips, chocolate-covered raisins, toffee bits or any of your cookie monsters' favorite candy pieces for the candy-coated chocolate pieces.*

Color-Bright Ice Cream Sandwiches

What you need:

¾ cup (1½ sticks) butter or margarine, softened
¾ cup creamy peanut butter
1¼ cups firmly packed light brown sugar
1 large egg
1 teaspoon vanilla extract
1½ cups all-purpose flour
1 teaspoon baking soda
¼ teaspoon salt
1¾ cups "M&M's"® Chocolate Mini Baking Bits, divided
2 quarts vanilla or chocolate ice cream, slightly softened

1 Preheat oven to 350°F.

2 In large bowl cream butter, peanut butter and sugar until light and fluffy; beat in egg and vanilla.

3 In medium bowl combine flour, baking soda and salt; blend into creamed mixture. Stir in *1⅓ cups "M&M's"® Chocolate Mini Baking Bits.*

4 Shape dough into 1¼-inch balls. Place about 2 inches apart on ungreased cookie sheets. Gently flatten to about ½-inch thickness with fingertips. Place 7 or 8 of the remaining *"M&M's"® Chocolate Mini Baking Bits* on each cookie; press in lightly.

5 Bake 10 to 12 minutes or until edges are light brown. *Do not overbake.* Cool about 1 minute on cookie sheets; cool completely on wire racks. Assemble cookies in pairs with about ⅓ cup ice cream; press cookies together lightly. Wrap each sandwich in plastic wrap; freeze until firm.
Makes about 24 ice cream sandwiches

Color-Bright Ice Cream Sandwiches

Child's Play

Chocolate Surprise Cookies

2¾ cups all-purpose flour
¾ cup unsweetened cocoa
   powder
½ teaspoon baking powder
½ teaspoon baking soda
1 cup (1 stick) butter,
   softened
1½ cups packed light brown
   sugar
½ cup plus 1 tablespoon
   granulated sugar,
   divided
2 eggs
1 teaspoon vanilla
1 cup chopped pecans,
   divided
1 package (9 ounces)
   caramels coated in milk
   chocolate
3 squares (1 ounce each)
   white chocolate,
   coarsely chopped

1 Preheat oven to 375°F.

2 Combine flour, cocoa, baking powder and baking soda in medium bowl; set aside.

3 Beat butter, brown sugar and ½ cup granulated sugar with electric mixer at medium speed until light and fluffy; beat in eggs and vanilla.

Gradually add flour mixture and ½ cup pecans; beat well. Cover dough; refrigerate 15 minutes or until firm enough to roll into balls.

4 Place remaining ½ cup pecans and 1 tablespoon sugar in shallow dish. Roll tablespoonful of dough around 1 caramel candy, covering completely; press one side into nut mixture. Place, nut side up, on ungreased cookie sheet. Repeat with additional dough and candies, placing cookies 3 inches apart.

5 Bake 10 to 12 minutes or until set and slightly cracked. Let stand on cookie sheet 2 minutes. Transfer cookies to wire rack; cool completely.

6 Place white chocolate pieces in small resealable plastic freezer bag; seal bag. Microwave at MEDIUM (50% power) 2 minutes. Turn bag over; microwave 2 to 3 minutes or until melted. Knead bag until chocolate is smooth. Cut off tiny corner of bag; drizzle chocolate onto cookies. Let stand about 30 minutes or until chocolate is set.

*Makes about
3½ dozen cookies*

Cookie Dough Art

Mini Pizza Cookies

What you need:

1 (20-ounce) tube of
  refrigerated sugar
  cookie dough
2 cups (16 ounces) prepared
  pink frosting
 "M&M's"® Chocolate Mini
  Baking Bits
 Variety of additional
  toppings such as
  shredded coconut,
  granola, raisins, nuts,
  small pretzels, snack
  mixes, sunflower seeds,
  popped corn and mini
  marshmallows

1 Preheat oven to 350°F.
Lightly grease cookie
sheets; set aside.

2 Divide dough into 8 equal
portions. On lightly floured
surface, roll each portion of
dough into ¼-inch-thick circle;
place about 2 inches apart onto
prepared cookie sheets.

3 Bake 10 to 13 minutes or
until golden brown on
edges. Cool completely on wire
racks. Spread top of each pizza
with frosting; sprinkle with
"M&M's"® Chocolate Mini Baking
Bits and 2 or 3 suggested
toppings.   *Makes 8 cookies*

16

Mini Pizza Cookies

Playing Card Cookies

What you need:

1 package (about 18 ounces) refrigerated sugar cookie dough
All-purpose flour (optional)

DECORATIONS

Cookie Glaze (recipe follows)
Assorted colored icings

1 Preheat oven to 350°F. Grease cookie sheets.

2 Remove dough from wrapper according to package directions. Divide dough into 2 equal sections. Reserve 1 section; cover and refrigerate remaining section.

3 Roll reserved section on lightly floured surface to ¼-inch thickness. Sprinkle with flour to minimize sticking, if necessary. Cut out 3½×2½-inch rectangles with sharp knife. Place cookies 2 inches apart on prepared cookie sheets. Repeat steps with remaining dough.

4 Bake 8 to 10 minutes or until edges are lightly browned. Remove from oven and straighten cookie edges with spatula. Cool on cookie sheets 2 minutes. Remove to wire racks; cool completely.

5 Place cookies on wire racks set over waxed paper. Spread Cookie Glaze over cookies. Let stand at room temperature 40 minutes or until glaze is set. Pipe colored icings onto cookies to resemble various playing card designs.

Makes about 26 cookies

Cookie Glaze

4 cups powdered sugar
4 to 6 tablespoons milk

1 Combine powdered sugar and enough milk, one tablespoon at a time, to make a medium-thick pourable glaze.

Peanut Butter and Jelly Sandwich Cookies

1 package (about 18 ounces) refrigerated sugar cookie dough
1 tablespoon unsweetened cocoa powder
All-purpose flour (optional)

FILLINGS
1¾ cups creamy peanut butter
½ cup grape jam or jelly

1 Remove dough from wrapper according to package directions. Reserve ¼ section of dough; cover and refrigerate remaining ¾ section of dough. Combine reserved dough and cocoa in small bowl; refrigerate.

2 Shape remaining ¾ section of dough into 5½-inch log. Sprinkle with flour to minimize sticking, if necessary. Remove chocolate dough from refrigerator; roll on sheet of waxed paper to 9½×6½-inch rectangle. Place dough log in center of rectangle.

3 Bring chocolate dough and waxed paper edges up and together over log. Press gently on top and sides of dough so entire log is wrapped in chocolate dough. Flatten log slightly to form square. Wrap in waxed paper. Freeze 10 minutes.

4 Preheat oven to 350°F.

5 Remove waxed paper. Cut log into ¼-inch slices. Place slices 2 inches apart on ungreased cookie sheets. Reshape dough edges into a square, if necessary. Press dough slightly to form indentations so dough resembles slice of bread.

6 Bake 8 to 11 minutes or until lightly browned. Remove from oven and straighten cookie edges with spatula. Cool 2 minutes on cookie sheets. Remove to wire racks; cool completely.

7 To make sandwich, spread about 1 tablespoon peanut butter on underside of 1 cookie. Spread about ½ tablespoon jam over peanut butter; top with second cookie, pressing gently. Repeat with remaining cookies.

Makes 11 sandwich cookies

Kitty Cookies

What you need:

1 package (about 18 ounces) refrigerated sugar cookie dough or desired flavor
All-purpose flour (optional)

DECORATIONS
White Decorator Frosting (recipe follows)
Assorted colored icings, colored candies and red licorice

1 Preheat oven to 350°F.

2 Remove dough from wrapper according to package directions. Divide dough into 2 equal sections. Reserve 1 section; cover and refrigerate remaining section.

3 Roll reserved dough on lightly floured surface to ⅛-inch thickness. Sprinkle with flour to minimize sticking, if necessary.

4 Cut out cookies using 3½-inch kitty face cookie cutter. Place cookies 2 inches apart on ungreased cookie sheets. Repeat with remaining dough.

5 Bake 8 to 10 minutes or until firm but not browned. Cool on cookie sheets 2 minutes. Remove to wire rack; cool completely.

6 Decorate with white and colored icings and candies as shown in photo.

Makes about 20 cookies

White Decorator Frosting

4 cups powdered sugar
½ cup vegetable shortening or unsalted butter
1 tablespoon corn syrup
6 to 8 tablespoons milk
Assorted paste food colorings

1 Beat sugar, shortening, corn syrup and milk in medium bowl at high speed of electric mixer 2 minutes or until fluffy. Add food colorings to achieve desired colors.

Under the Sea

1 package (about 18
    ounces) refrigerated
    sugar cookie dough
Blue liquid or paste food
    coloring
All-purpose flour
    (optional)

DECORATIONS

Blue Royal Icing (recipe
    follows)
Assorted small decors,
    gummy candies and
    hard candies

1 Preheat oven to 350°F.
    Grease 12-inch pizza pan.

2 Remove dough from
    wrapper according to
package directions. Combine
dough and blue food coloring,
a few drops at a time, in large
bowl until desired color is
achieved; blend until smooth.

3 Press dough into bottom
    of prepared pan, leaving
about ¾-inch space between
edge of dough and pan.
Sprinkle dough with flour to
minimize sticking, if necessary.

4 Bake 10 to 12 minutes or
    until set in center. Cool
completely in pan on wire rack.

Run spatula between cookie
crust and pan after 10 to 15
minutes to loosen.

5 Spread Blue Royal Icing
    randomly over cookie to
resemble texture of sea. Once
icing is set, decorate with
decors and candies as shown
in photo.

Makes 10 to 12 wedges

Blue Royal Icing

1 egg white,* at room
    temperature
2 to 2½ cups sifted
    powdered sugar
½ teaspoon almond extract
Blue liquid or paste food
    coloring

*Use clean, uncracked egg.

1 Beat egg white in small
    bowl at high speed of
electric mixer until foamy.

2 Gradually add 2 cups
    powdered sugar and
almond extract. Beat at low
speed until moistened. Increase
mixer speed to high and beat
until icing is stiff, adding
additional powdered sugar
if needed. Tint icing blue with
food coloring, a few drops at a
time, until desired color is
achieved.

Dude Ranch

What you need:

1 package (about 18 ounces) refrigerated sugar cookie dough
All-purpose flour (optional)

DECORATIONS
Royal Icing (page 28)
Assorted food colorings, fruit chews, small decors and hard candies
12 (4×3-inch) frosted chocolate toaster pastries
35 (7½-inch) pretzel rods

SUPPLIES
Cardboard, decorative paper and plastic wrap

1 Draw patterns for cowboys and horses on cardboard using diagrams on page 28; cut out patterns.

2 Preheat oven to 350°F. Grease cookie sheets.

3 Remove dough from wrapper according to package directions. Divide dough into 2 equal sections. Reserve 1 section; cover and refrigerate remaining section.

4 Roll reserved dough on lightly floured surface to ¼-inch thickness. Sprinkle with flour to minimize sticking, if necessary. Lay sheet of waxed paper over dough. Place patterns over waxed paper. Cut dough around patterns with sharp knife; remove patterns and waxed paper. Place cookies 2 inches apart on prepared cookie sheets. Repeat with remaining dough.

5 Bake 10 to 12 minutes or until edges are lightly browned. Remove from oven. Cool on cookie sheets 2 minutes. Remove to wire racks; cool completely.

6 Prepare Royal Icing. Tint about 1 cup icing to match color of toaster pastries used for corral floor. Tint small amounts of remaining icing with desired food colors to decorate cowboys and horses; place in small resealable plastic food storage bags. Cut off small corners of bags for piping.

7 Decorate cowboys and horses with colored sugars, decors and hard candies as shown in photo.

continued on page 28

Dude Ranch

Dude Ranch, *continued*

8 Cover 20×12-inch piece of cardboard with decorative paper and plastic wrap. Assemble corral floor by placing cardboard with 12-inch side facing you. Pipe icing on bottom of toaster pastries; place vertically, 4 down and 3 across, in center of cardboard.

9 Assemble fence by carefully cutting 5 pretzel rods into 3 equal sections with serrated knife. Pipe icing down 1 whole pretzel rod and 1 cut pretzel rod. Place end to end to fit 12-inch side of corral. Repeat at other 12-inch side. Pipe icing down 1 cut pretzel rod and 2 whole pretzel rods. Place end to end to fit 20-inch side of corral. Pipe icing down 2 whole rods. Place at other 20-inch side, leaving opening for entrance. Continue building fence with 4 additional layers on each side. Let dry. Pipe icing on feet of cowboys and horses; arrange so they can be supported by fence or each other.   *Makes 1 fence and 16 cookies*

Royal Icing

2 egg whites*
**4 to 4½ cups sifted
  powdered sugar
1 teaspoon almond extract**

*Use clean, uncracked eggs.

1 Beat egg whites in medium bowl at high speed of electric mixer until foamy.

2 Gradually add 4 cups powdered sugar and almond extract. Beat at low speed until moistened. Increase mixer speed to high and beat until icing is stiff, adding additional powdered sugar if needed.

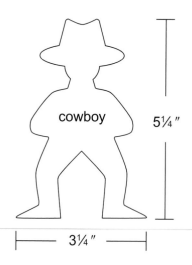

cowboy   5¼ ″

3¼ ″

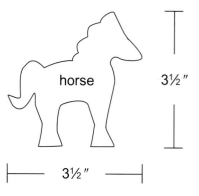

horse   3½ ″

3½ ″

Choo-choo Train

1 package (about 18 ounces) refrigerated peanut butter cookie dough or desired flavor
All-purpose flour (optional)

DECORATIONS
   Purple Cookie Glaze (page 30)
   Assorted colored icings, colored candies, small decors and 2 small peanut butter sandwich crackers

SUPPLIES
   Cardboard

1 Draw patterns for 4 train cars on cardboard, using diagrams on page 30; cut out patterns.

2 Preheat oven to 350°F. Line cookie sheets with parchment paper.

3 Remove dough from wrapper according to package directions. Roll dough on lightly floured surface to 18×13-inch rectangle. Sprinkle with flour to minimize sticking, if necessary. Place on prepared cookie sheet.

4 Bake 8 to 10 minutes or until lightly browned. Cool on baking sheet 5 minutes. Slide cookie and parchment paper onto wire rack; cool 5 minutes.

5 While still warm, lay sheet of waxed paper over cookie. Place patterns over waxed paper. Cut cookie around patterns with sharp knife; remove patterns and waxed paper. Cover with towel; cool completely.

6 Spread Purple Cookie Glaze on train cars as shown in photo. Allow glaze to set about 30 minutes before decorating. Decorate with icings, candy and decors as shown in photo. Use peanut butter sandwich crackers as large train wheels. Assemble train on board or platter.

Makes 1 (4-car) train cookie

continued on page 30

Choo-choo Train, continued

Purple Cookie Glaze
2 cups powdered sugar
7 to 9 tablespoons heavy cream, divided
Liquid or paste food colorings

1 Combine powdered sugar and 6 tablespoons cream in medium bowl; whisk until smooth. Add enough remaining cream, 1 tablespoon at a time, to make a medium-thick pourable glaze. Tint icing purple with food coloring, a few drops at a time, until desired color is achieved.

Makes 1 cup glaze

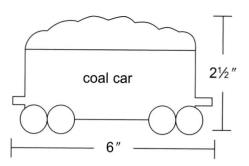

coal car

2½"

6"

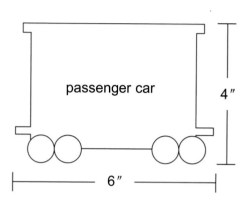

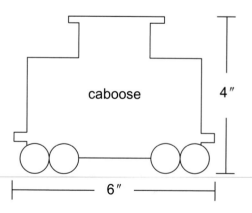

passenger car

4"

6"

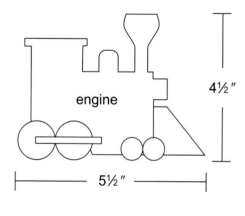

engine

4½"

5½"

caboose

4"

6"

Lollipop Clowns

1 package (about 18 ounces) refrigerated red, green or blue cookie dough*
All-purpose flour (optional)

DECORATIONS
Assorted colored icings and hard candies

SUPPLIES
18 (4-inch) lollipop sticks

*If colored dough is unavailable, sugar cookie dough can be tinted with paste food colorings.

1 Preheat oven to 350°F.

2 Remove dough from wrapper according to package directions. Divide dough into 2 equal sections. Reserve 1 section; cover and refrigerate remaining section.

3 Roll reserved dough on lightly floured surface to ⅛-inch thickness. Sprinkle with flour to minimize sticking, if necessary.

4 Cut out cookies using 3½-inch round cookie cutter. Place lollipop sticks on cookies so that tips of sticks are imbedded in cookies. Carefully turn cookies so sticks are in back; place on ungreased cookie sheets.

5 Bake 8 to 10 minutes or until firm but not brown. Cool on cookie sheets 2 minutes. Remove to wire racks; cool completely.

6 Decorate cookies with icings as shown in photo.
Makes about 18 cookies

Tip: *These happy clown faces make the perfect topping for a birthday cake. Stick a Lollipop Clown, one for each child, in the cake for a wonderful circus theme party.*

Cookie Tools

What you need:

1 package (about 18 ounces) refrigerated chocolate cookie dough*
All-purpose flour (optional)

DECORATIONS
White Decorator Frosting (page 36)
Assorted colored sprinkles and colored frostings

SUPPLIES
Cardboard

*If refrigerated chocolate cookie dough is unavailable, add ¼ cup unsweetened cocoa powder to refrigerated sugar cookie dough. Beat in large bowl at high speed of electric mixer until will blended.

1 Draw patterns for tools on cardboard, using diagrams on page 36; cut out patterns.

2 Preheat oven to 350°F.

3 Remove dough from wrapper according to package directions. Divide dough into 2 equal sections. Reserve 1 section; cover and refrigerate remaining section.

4 Roll reserved dough on lightly floured surface to ⅛-inch thickness. Sprinkle with flour to minimize sticking, if necessary.

5 Lay sheet of waxed paper over dough. Place patterns over waxed paper. Cut dough around patterns with sharp knife; remove patterns and waxed paper. Place cookies 2 inches apart on ungreased cookie sheets. Repeat with remaining dough and any scraps.

6 Bake 8 to 10 minutes or until firm, but not browned. Cool on cookie sheets 2 minutes. Remove to wire rack; cool completely.

7 Spread frosting evenly over top of each cookie. Decorate with sprinkles and frostings. *Makes about 2 dozen cookies*

continued on page 36

Cookie Tools, continued

White Decorator Frosting

1 pound powdered sugar
½ cup vegetable shortening
or unsalted butter
1 tablespoon corn syrup
6 to 8 tablespoons milk
Assorted paste food
colorings

1 Beat sugar, shortening, corn syrup and milk in medium bowl at high speed of electric mixer 2 minutes or until fluffy. Add food colorings to achieve desired colors.

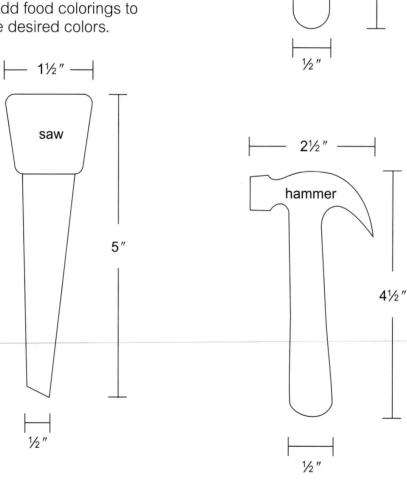

wrench

1½″

5″

½″

saw

1½″

5″

½″

hammer

2½″

4½″

½″

"Radical" Peanut Butter Pizza Cookies

What you need:

COOKIES
1 Butter Flavor* CRISCO® Stick or 1 cup Butter Flavor CRISCO® all-vegetable shortening
1¼ cups granulated sugar, divided
1 cup packed dark brown sugar
1 cup creamy peanut butter
2 eggs
1 teaspoon baking soda
1 teaspoon vanilla
½ teaspoon salt
2 cups all-purpose flour
2 cups quick oats, uncooked

PIZZA SAUCE
2 cups milk chocolate chips
¼ Butter Flavor* CRISCO® Stick or ¼ cup Butter Flavor CRISCO® all-vegetable shortening

PIZZA TOPPINGS (page 38)

DRIZZLE
1 cup chopped white confectionery coating

*Butter Flavor Crisco is artificially flavored.

1 Heat oven to 350°F. Place sheets of foil on countertop for cooling cookies.

2 For cookies, combine shortening, 1 cup granulated sugar and brown sugar in large bowl. Beat at low speed of electric mixer until well blended. Add peanut butter, eggs, baking soda, vanilla and salt. Mix about 2 minutes or until well blended. Stir in flour and oats with spoon.

3 Place remaining ¼ cup granulated sugar in small bowl.

4 Measure ¼ cup dough. Shape into ball. Repeat with remaining dough. Roll each ball in sugar. Place 4 inches apart on ungreased cookie sheets. Flatten into 4-inch circles.

5 Bake at 350°F for 8 to 10 minutes. *Do not overbake.* Use back of spoon to flatten center and up to edge of each hot cookie to resemble pizza crust. Cool 5 to 8 minutes on baking sheet. Remove pizza to foil to cool completely.

6 For pizza sauce, combine chocolate chips and shortening in large microwave-safe measuring cup or bowl.

continued on page 38

"Radical" Peanut Butter Pizza Cookies, continued

Microwave at MEDIUM (50%) 2 to 3 minutes or until chips are shiny and soft (or melt on rangetop in small saucepan on very low heat). Stir until smooth. Spoon 2 teaspoons melted chocolate into center of each cookie. Spread to inside edge. Sprinkle desired toppings over chocolate.

7 For drizzle, place chopped confectionery coating in heavy resealable plastic food storage bag. Seal. Microwave at MEDIUM (50%). Knead bag after 1 minute. Repeat until smooth (or melt by placing in bowl of hot water). Cut pinpoint hole in corner of bag. Squeeze out and drizzle over cookies.

Makes about 2 dozen cookies

PIZZA TOPPINGS
Mmmmm: candy coated chocolate pieces
Beary good: gummy bears
Jumbo jewels: small pieces of gumdrops
Bubble gum-like: round sprinkles and balls
German chocolate: chopped pecans and flake coconut
Cherries jubilee: candied cherries and slivered almonds

Rocky road: miniature marshmallows and mini semisweet chocolate chips
Harvest mix: candy corn and chopped peanuts
Ants and logs: cashews and raisins

Tip: These cookies are a great project for kids' parties and rainy days. Premake the cookies and let the children create their own cookie pizzas.

"Radical" Peanut Butter Pizza Cookies

CREATIVE COOKIE CENTER

Moons and Stars

What you need:

1 cup (2 sticks) butter, softened
1 cup sugar
1 egg
2 teaspoons lemon peel
½ teaspoon almond extract
3 cups all-purpose flour
½ cup ground almonds
    All-purpose flour
    (optional)

DECORATIONS
    Assorted colored icings, hard candies and colored sprinkles

1 Preheat oven to 350°F. Grease cookie sheets. Beat butter, sugar, egg, lemon peel and almond extract in large bowl at medium speed of electric mixer until fluffy.

2 Combine flour and almonds in medium bowl. Add to butter mixture; mix only to incorporate flour.

3 Roll dough on lightly floured surface to ¼-inch thickness. Cut out cookies using cookie cutters. Place 2 inches apart on cookie sheets.

4 Bake 7 to 9 minutes or until set. Cool on cookie sheets 2 minutes. Remove to wire rack; cool completely. Decorate. *Makes about 4 dozen cookies*

40

Crayon Cookies

What you need:

1 cup (2 sticks) butter, softened
2 teaspoons vanilla
½ cup powdered sugar
2¼ cups all-purpose flour
¼ teaspoon salt
Assorted paste food colorings

DECORATIONS
1½ cups chocolate chips
1½ teaspoons shortening

1 Preheat oven to 350°F. Grease cookie sheets.

2 Beat butter and vanilla in large bowl at high speed of electric mixer until fluffy. Add sugar; beat at medium speed until blended. Combine flour and salt in small bowl. Gradually add to butter mixture.

3 Divide dough into 10 equal sections. Reserve 1 section; cover and refrigerate remaining 9 sections. Combine reserved section and desired food coloring in small bowl; blend well.

4 Cut dough into 2 equal sections. Roll each section into 5-inch log. Pinch one end to resemble crayon tip. Place cookies 2 inches apart on prepared cookie sheets. Repeat with remaining 9 sections of dough and desired food colorings.

5 Bake 15 to 18 minutes or until edges are lightly browned. Cool completely on cookie sheets.

6 Combine chocolate chips and shortening in small microwavable bowl. Microwave on HIGH 1 to 1½ minutes, stirring after 1 minute, or until smooth. Decorate with chocolate mixture as shown in photo.
Makes 20 cookies

Lady Bugs

¾ **cup shortening**
½ **cup sugar**
¼ **cup honey**
 1 **egg**
½ **teaspoon vanilla**
 2 **cups all-purpose flour**
⅓ **cup cornmeal**
 1 **teaspoon baking powder**
½ **teaspoon salt**

DECORATIONS
**Orange and black icings
and yellow candy-
coated pieces**

1 Beat shortening, sugar and honey in large bowl at medium speed of electric mixer until light and fluffy. Add egg and vanilla; mix until well blended.

2 Combine flour, cornmeal, baking powder and salt in medium bowl. Add to shortening mixture; mix at low speed until blended. Cover; refrigerate several hours or overnight, if desired.

3 Preheat oven to 375°F.

4 Divide dough into 24 equal sections. Shape each section into 2×1¼-inch oval-shaped ball. Place balls 2 inches apart on ungreased cookie sheets.

5 Bake 10 to 12 minutes or until lightly browned. Cool on cookie sheets 2 minutes. Remove to wire rack; cool completely.

6 Decorate cookies with icings and candies as shown in photo.
Makes 2 dozen cookies

Sunflower Cookies in Flowerpots

What you need:

Butter Cookie dough
(page 48)
1 container (16 ounces)
vanilla frosting
Yellow food coloring
Powdered sugar
1 gallon ice cream (any
flavor), softened
Brown decorating icing
24 chocolate sandwich
cookies, crushed
1 cup shredded coconut,
tinted green*

SUPPLIES
12 (6-inch) lollipop sticks
6 plastic drinking straws
12 (6½-ounce) paper cups
Pastry bag and small
writing tip
12 new (3¼-inch-diameter)
ceramic flowerpots,
about 3½ inches tall

*See Tinting Coconut, page 5.

1 Preheat oven to 350°F.
Grease cookie sheets.

2 Prepare Butter Cookie
dough. Roll dough on
lightly-floured surface to ⅛-inch
thickness. Cut out cookies with
fluted cookie cutter; place on
prepared cookie sheets.

3 Bake 8 to 10 minutes or
until edges are lightly
browned. Remove to wire racks;
cool completely.

4 Color vanilla frosting with
yellow food coloring.
Measure out ⅔ cup colored
frosting; cover and set aside
remaining frosting. Blend
enough additional powdered
sugar into measured ⅔ cup
frosting to make very thick
frosting. Use about 1 tablespoon
thickened frosting to attach
lollipop stick to back of each
cookie. Set aside to allow
frosting to dry completely.

5 Cut straws crosswise in
half. Hold 1 straw upright
in center of each cup; pack ice
cream around straw, completely
filling each cup with ice cream.
(Be sure straw sticks up out of
ice cream.) Freeze until ice
cream is hardened, 3 to 4 hours.

continued on page 48

*Sunflower Cookies
in Flowerpots*

**Sunflower Cookies in
Flowerpots, continued**

6 Frost front side of each
cookie as desired with
remaining frosting. Spoon brown
icing into pastry bag fitted with
writing tip; use to decorate
cookies as shown in photo.

7 To serve, place cups filled
with ice cream in
flowerpots. Top with cookie
crumbs to resemble dirt.
Sprinkle tinted coconut around
straw to resemble grass. Clip
straw off to make it even with
ice cream, taking care not to fill
straw with crumbs or coconut.
Insert lollipop stick, with cookie
attached, into opening in each
straw to stand cookie upright in
flowerpot.
Makes 12 servings

Butter Cookie Dough
¾ **cup butter, softened**
¼ **cup granulated sugar**
¼ **cup packed light brown
      sugar**
 1 **egg yolk**
1¾ **cups all-purpose flour**
 ¾ **teaspoon baking powder**
 ⅛ **teaspoon salt**

1 Combine butter, granulated
sugar, brown sugar and
egg yolk in medium bowl. Add
flour, baking powder and salt;
mix well.

2 Cover; refrigerate about
4 hours or until firm.

*Tip: To create a summer flower
cookie garden, pair these
Sunflower Cookies in Flowerpots with
a batch of Lady Bugs (page 44) and
beautiful Butterfly Cookies (page 52).*

Chocolate Lattice Cookie Baskets

What you need:

¾ cup sugar
½ cup (1 stick) butter, softened
1 egg
1 teaspoon vanilla
2½ cups all-purpose flour
½ cup unsweetened cocoa powder
½ teaspoon baking powder
¼ teaspoon salt
½ cup sour cream

DECORATIONS

Brown Royal Icing (page 50)
4 red licorice twists
Assorted candies

1 Beat sugar and butter in large bowl at high speed of electric mixer until light and fluffy. Add egg and vanilla; mix until blended.

2 Combine flour, cocoa, baking powder and salt in medium bowl. Add half flour mixture to butter mixture; mix at low speed until well blended. Add sour cream; mix well. Add remaining flour mixture; mix well. Divide dough into 2 equal sections. Cover and refrigerate several hours or overnight.

3 Roll 1 section of dough on well-floured surface to ¼-inch thickness. Transfer to parchment-lined cookie sheet. Cut dough into 8×7-inch rectangle. Reserve scraps. With 8-inch side facing you, cut lengthwise into 8×5-inch piece and 8×2-inch piece. Place pieces horizontally with larger piece above smaller piece.

4 Leaving ½-inch uncut border at top edge of 8×5-inch piece, vertically cut into 16 (½-inch-wide) equal strips. Cut 8×2-inch piece horizontally into 4 (½-inch-wide) equal strips. Cover and refrigerate 10 minutes.

5 Place 8×5-inch piece with strips facing you vertically. Beginning on your left, fold every other strip back and over the top border.

6 Place 1 strip from 8×2-inch piece horizontally across unfolded strips. Unfold strips back to their original position.

7 Beginning with the second vertical strip on your left, fold every other strip back. Insert another horizontal strip as directed in step 6. Repeat with remaining 2 horizontal strips.

continued on page 50

Chocolate Lattice Cookie Baskets, continued

8 Cut off ½-inch top border. Flatten lattice slightly with palm of hand. Straighten edges with spatula so lattice measures 8×4 inches, if necessary. Chill 10 minutes.

9 Preheat oven to 350°F.

10 Cut lattice into eight 2-inch squares. Roll reserved scraps on lightly floured surface to ¼-inch thickness. Cut two 2¼-inch squares. Place on cookie sheet with lattice.

11 Bake 15 to 17 minutes or until set. Cool completely on cookie sheet set on wire rack. Repeat steps 3 through 11 with remaining dough.

12 Place icing in small resealable plastic food storage bag; cut off small corner of bag.

13 Lightly grease parchment or waxed paper cut to fit large cookie sheet or tray. Place one 2¼-inch-square basket bottom on parchment paper. Pipe icing on edges of 3 sides of lattice squares. Position lattice squares to form 4 sided box, leaving plain sides at top.

Place small cups against outer sides to hold in place until set. Pipe a small amount of icing to ends of 1 licorice twist. Press licorice ends into opposite basket seams to create a handle. Let stand at least 4 hours before filling. Repeat steps with remaining cookie basket pieces.

Makes 4 baskets

Brown Royal Icing

1 egg white, at room temperature
2 to 2½ cups sifted powdered sugar
½ teaspoon almond extract
Assorted liquid or paste food colorings

1 Beat egg white in small bowl at high speed of electric mixer until foamy.

2 Gradually add 2 cups powdered sugar and almond extract. Beat at low speed until moistened. Increase speed to high and beat until icing is stiff, adding additional powdered sugar if needed. Tint with food colorings until a shade of brown that matches lattice dough is achieved.

Chocolate Lattice Cookie Baskets

Butterfly Cookies

2¼ cups all-purpose flour
¼ teaspoon salt
1 cup sugar
¾ cup (1½ sticks) butter,
    softened
1 egg
1 teaspoon vanilla
1 teaspoon almond extract

DECORATIONS

**White frosting, assorted
food colorings, colored
sugars, assorted small
decors, gummy fruit and
hard candies**

1 Combine flour and salt in medium bowl; set aside.

2 Beat sugar and butter in large bowl at medium speed of electric mixer until fluffy. Beat in egg, vanilla and almond extract. Gradually add flour mixture. Beat at low speed until well blended.

3 Divide dough into 2 equal sections. Cover; refrigerate 30 minutes or until firm.

4 Preheat oven to 350°F. Grease cookie sheets.

5 Reserve 1 section; cover and refrigerate remaining section. Roll reserved dough on lightly floured surface to ¼-inch thickness. Cut out cookies using butterfly cookie cutters. Repeat with remaining dough.

6 Bake 12 to 15 minutes or until edges are lightly browned. Remove to wire racks; cool completely.

7 Tint portions of white frosting with assorted food colorings. Spread desired color of frosting over cookie. Repeat with remaining cookies.

8 Decorate with colored sugars, assorted small decors, gummy fruit and hard candies as desired.

*Makes about
20 to 22 cookies*

Butterfly Cookies

Peanut Butter Bears

What you need:

1 cup **SKIPPY®** **Creamy Peanut Butter**
1 cup (2 sticks) **MAZOLA® Margarine or butter, softened**
1 cup **packed brown sugar**
⅔ cup **KARO® Light or Dark Corn Syrup**
2 **eggs**
4 cups **flour, divided**
1 tablespoon **baking powder**
1 teaspoon **cinnamon (optional)**
¼ teaspoon **salt**

1 In large bowl with mixer at medium speed, beat peanut butter, margarine, brown sugar, corn syrup and eggs until smooth. Reduce speed; beat in 2 cups of flour, baking powder, cinnamon and salt. With spoon, stir in remaining 2 cups flour. Wrap dough in plastic wrap; refrigerate 2 hours.

2 Preheat oven to 325°F. Divide dough in half; set aside half.

3 On floured surface roll out half the dough to ⅛-inch thickness. Cut with floured bear cookie cutter. Repeat with remaining dough.

4 Use scraps of dough to make bear faces. Make one small ball of dough for muzzle. Form 3 smaller balls of dough and press gently to create eyes and nose; bake as directed.

5 Bake bears on ungreased cookie sheets 10 minutes or until lightly browned. Remove from cookie sheets; cool completely on wire rack. Decorate as desired, using frosting to create paws, ears and bow ties. *Makes about 3 dozen bears*

Baseball Caps

1 cup (2 sticks) butter, softened
7 ounces almond paste
¾ cup sugar
1 egg
1 teaspoon vanilla
¼ teaspoon salt
3 cups all-purpose flour

DECORATIONS

Assorted colored icings and colored candies

1 Preheat oven to 350°F. Grease cookie sheets.

2 Beat butter, almond paste, sugar, egg, vanilla and salt in large bowl at high speed of electric mixer until light and fluffy. Add flour all at once; stir just to combine.

3 Roll ¼ of dough on lightly floured surface to ⅛-inch thickness. Cut out 1-inch circles. Place circles 2 inches apart on prepared cookie sheets.

4 Roll remaining dough into 1-inch balls. Place one ball on top of half dough circle so about ½ inch of circle sticks out to form bill of baseball cap.

5 Bake 10 to 12 minutes or until lightly browned. If bills brown too quickly, cut small strips of foil and cover with shiny side of foil facing you. Cool on cookie sheet 2 minutes. Remove to wire rack; cool completely.

6 Decorate with icings and candies as shown in photo.
Makes about 3 dozen cookies

Tip: *Using a 1-tablespoon scoop is a great way to keep the baseball caps uniform in size and professional looking.*

Caramel Lizard Cookies

What you need:

½ cup shortening
⅓ cup packed light brown
    sugar
¼ cup dark molasses
1 egg white
½ teaspoon vanilla
1½ to 2 cups all-purpose flour
1 teaspoon ground
    cinnamon
½ teaspoon baking soda
½ teaspoon salt
½ teaspoon ground ginger
¼ teaspoon baking powder

DECORATIONS

1 bag (14 ounces) caramels,
    unwrapped
2 tablespoons milk
1 cup walnut chips
    Mini-chocolate chips,
    granola or mini
    chocolate candy-coated
    pieces
    Red licorice string, cut
    into ¾-inch pieces
    Chocolate sprinkles

SUPPLIES

Cardboard

1 Draw pattern for lizard on cardboard, using diagram on page 60; cut out pattern.

2 Beat shortening, brown sugar, molasses, egg white and vanilla in large bowl at high speed of electric mixer until smooth.

3 Combine 1½ cups flour, cinnamon, baking soda, salt, ginger and baking powder in small bowl. Add to shortening mixture; mix well. Add additional flour, if needed. Cover; refrigerate about 8 hours or until firm.

4 Preheat oven to 350°F. Grease cookie sheets.

5 Divide dough into 4 equal sections. Reserve 1 section; cover and refrigerate remaining 3 sections. Roll reserved dough into circle on lightly floured surface to ¼-inch thickness.

6 Lay sheet of waxed paper over dough. Place pattern over waxed paper. Cut dough with sharp knife; remove pattern and waxed paper. Place cookies on prepared cookie sheets. Repeat with remaining dough.

7 Bake 9 to 11 minutes or until set. Cool on cookie sheets 5 minutes. Remove to wire racks; cool completely.

continued on page 60

Caramel Lizard Cookies

Caramel Lizard cookies, continued

8 Melt caramels and milk in small saucepan over low heat, stirring frequently, until smooth. Keep saucepan over very low heat while decorating cookies.

9 Place cookies on sheet of waxed paper. Spread caramel evenly over top of lizards. Decorate with walnuts, chocolate chips, cereal, candy and sprinkles as shown in photo. *Makes about 20 cookies*

Tip: It's easy to create the perfect reptile theme party. Simply pair together these chewy Caramel Lizard Cookies and Brownie Turtle Cookies (page 8) for a great creepy crawly hit.

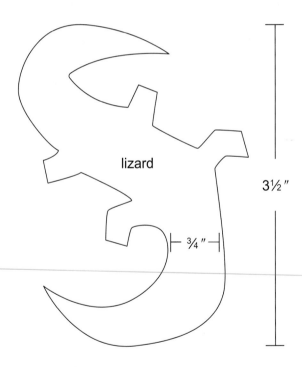

lizard

3½ "

¾ "

INDEX

ACKNOWLEDGMENTS

The publishers would like to thank the companies and organizations listed below for the use of their recipes and photographs in this publication.

Best Foods

Hershey Foods Corporation

M&M/MARS

The Procter & Gamble Company

NOTES

_____

_____

_____

_____

_____

_____

_____

_____

METRIC CONVERSION CHART

VOLUME MEASUREMENTS (dry)

⅛ teaspoon = 0.5 mL

¼ teaspoon = 1 mL

½ teaspoon = 2 mL

¾ teaspoon = 4 mL

1 teaspoon = 5 mL

1 tablespoon = 15 mL

2 tablespoons = 30 mL

¼ cup = 60 mL

⅓ cup = 75 mL

½ cup = 125 mL

⅔ cup = 150 mL

¾ cup = 175 mL

1 cup = 250 mL

2 cups = 1 pint = 500 mL

3 cups = 750 mL

4 cups = 1 quart = 1 L

VOLUME MEASUREMENTS (fluid)

1 fluid ounce (2 tablespoons) = 30 mL

4 fluid ounces (½ cup) = 125 mL

8 fluid ounces (1 cup) = 250 mL

12 fluid ounces (1½ cups) = 375 mL

16 fluid ounces (2 cups) = 500 mL

WEIGHTS (mass)

½ ounce = 15 g

1 ounce = 30 g

3 ounces = 90 g

4 ounces = 120 g

8 ounces = 225 g

10 ounces = 285 g

12 ounces = 360 g

16 ounces = 1 pound = 450 g

DIMENSIONS

1/16 inch = 2 mm

⅛ inch = 3 mm

¼ inch = 6 mm

½ inch = 1.5 cm

¾ inch = 2 cm

1 inch = 2.5 cm

OVEN TEMPERATURES

250°F = 120°C

275°F = 140°C

300°F = 150°C

325°F = 160°C

350°F = 180°C

375°F = 190°C

400°F = 200°C

425°F = 220°C

450°F = 230°C

BAKING PAN SIZES

Utensil	Size in Inches/ Quarts	Metric Volume	Size in Centimeters
Baking or Cake Pan (square or rectangular)	8×8×2	2 L	20×20×5
	9×9×2	2.5 L	23×23×5
	12×8×2	3 L	30×20×5
	13×9×2	3.5 L	33×23×5
Loaf Pan	8×4×3	1.5 L	20×10×7
	9×5×3	2 L	23×13×7
Round Layer Cake Pan	8×1½	1.2 L	20×4
	9×1½	1.5 L	23×4
Pie Plate	8×1¼	750 mL	20×3
	9×1¼	1 L	23×3
Baking Dish or Casserole	1 quart	1 L	—
	1½ quart	1.5 L	—
	2 quart	2 L	—